Children's Authors

Pam Muñoz Ryan

Jill C. Wheeler
ABDO Publishing Company

Published by ABDO Publishing Company, 8000 West 78th Street, Edina, Minnesota 55439.
Copyright © 2009 by Abdo Consulting Group, Inc. International copyrights reserved in all
countries. No part of this book may be reproduced in any form without written permission from the
publisher. The Checkerboard Library™ is a trademark and logo of ABDO Publishing Company.

Printed in the United States.

Cover Photo: Sean Masterson
Interior Photos: AP Images pp. 11, 15; Corbis p. 9; Getty Images pp. 7, 17; iStockphoto p. 13;
    Sean Masterson pp. 5, 19, 21

Editors: Tamara L. Britton, Megan M. Gunderson
Art Direction: Neil Klinepier

Library of Congress Cataloging-in-Publication Data

Wheeler, Jill C., 1964-
  Pam Muñoz Ryan / Jill C. Wheeler.
      p. cm. -- (Children's authors)
  Includes bibliographical references and index.
  ISBN 978-1-60453-078-0
  1. Ryan, Pam Muñoz--Juvenile literature. 2. Authors, American--20th century--Biography--
Juvenile literature. 3. Authors, American--21st century--Biography--Juvenile literature. I. Title.

  PS3568.Y3926Z95 2009
  818'.5409--dc22
  [B]
                                    2008004805

Contents

Pam Muñoz Ryan

Some readers may not be familiar with Pam Muñoz Ryan. However, they have probably heard of her work. She has written more than 30 picture books, novels, and nonfiction books for young readers.

Ryan has written about courageous heroines from different times in history. Her stories show women overcoming the challenges of race and **gender**. They include such award-winning titles as *Amelia and Eleanor Go for a Ride*, *When Marian Sang*, *Esperanza Rising*, and *Becoming Naomi León*.

When Ryan writes, she starts with a scene and continues from there. She does extensive research for each book. Writing can be a long and difficult process. Yet Ryan's fans will agree, the results are worth it!

Pam Muñoz Ryan

Family Ties

Pam Muñoz Ryan was born on December 25, 1951, in Bakersfield, California. Her parents are Don Bell and Esperanza "Hope" Muñoz. She is the oldest of three sisters.

Both of Pam's grandmothers lived near her family. Many of Pam's aunts and uncles lived nearby, too. On her mother's side of the family, Pam is also the oldest of 23 grandchildren. Pam enjoyed spending time with her relatives. Their gatherings were loud and lively!

Pam's grandmothers had lived through the **Great Depression**. They had both worked hard to overcome poverty. Yet, they were also very different. Pam's father's mother was from Oklahoma. Her mother's mother was from Mexico.

Pam's Mexican grandmother's name was Esperanza. She spoke to Pam in Spanish. Esperanza had come to the United States in the 1930s. In fact, Pam's mother had been born in a camp for Mexican farmworkers.

Pam's mother was born in a camp at DiGiorgio Farms, a fruit grower. In 1948, workers at the farm went on strike for better working conditions.

Escaping into Books

As a child, Pam had plenty of time to exercise her imagination. She loved to daydream, put on plays, and play games. Sometimes she pretended to be a queen! Other times she pretended to be an explorer or a doctor.

Pam also loved to read. She often went to the library during Bakersfield's long, hot summers. There, Pam could choose books in air-conditioned comfort!

Her favorite books included Laura Ingalls Wilder's Little House series. She also liked adventure stories such as Robert Louis Stevenson's *Treasure Island* and *The Swiss Family Robinson* by Johann David Wyss.

When she was in fifth grade, Pam's family moved to a different part of town. She felt out of place in her new school. So, Pam visited the library even more. She would ride her bike to the library and return with lots of books.

Though hot, Bakersfield's climate is perfect for producing solar power. The ARCO solar power plant outside the city has 756 solar panels that generate electricity for 2,300 homes.

Trying Out Teaching

Despite her love of books, Pam didn't think about becoming a writer. She held other jobs instead. Pam babysat and worked in a department store. She also worked as a secretary and as a teacher's assistant.

After graduating from high school, Pam attended San Diego State University (SDSU). There, she earned a **degree** in child development. Her first job was as a Head Start teacher. Pam was able to use both her English and Spanish language skills at Head Start.

Pam put her teaching career on hold when she married her husband, Jim. The Ryans eventually had four children. When her youngest children went to preschool, Pam returned to SDSU. This time, she earned a master's degree in education.

One of Pam's classes became a turning point in her career. One day, one of Pam's professors asked if she had ever thought about writing professionally. Pam had not. But the professor's comment started her thinking.

Head Start is a national program for children from low-income families.
They receive meals, health care, and learn educational and social skills.
These Head Start students say "Hello!" from San Diego, California.

First Chapters

After earning her master's **degree**, Ryan became the director of an early childhood program. However, she had not forgotten what her professor had said.

Just weeks later, a friend asked Ryan for help writing a book. Ryan ended up writing more books with her friend. All of these books were for adults.

Then, Ryan began writing stories for young readers. She received many rejection letters from publishers. But Ryan worked hard and **persevered**. Finally, a publisher agreed to publish one of Ryan's picture books.

Ryan's first book for children was published in 1994. In *One Hundred Is a Family*, different kinds of families help kids learn numbers. The book also shows that families are not limited to those that have a mother, a father, and children.

Ryan continued writing picture books. One day, Ryan saw the American flag displayed in a disrespectful manner. In response, Ryan wrote *The Flag We Love*. The book teaches readers about the flag's history and what it represents.

Ryan was upset to see the flag improperly displayed. Rules for displaying and caring for the flag are established by the United States Flag Code.

Blending Fact with Fiction

Ryan continued her writing career with several more picture books. One of them was the 1997 book *California Here We Come!* The book contains many surprising facts about Ryan's home state. It also led Ryan into a new **genre**, historical fiction.

While doing research for the California book, Ryan learned of a stagecoach driver called One-Eyed Charley. Charley was actually Charlotte Parkhurst, a woman who lived her life disguised as a man. She became the first woman to vote in a federal election. She did this more than 50 years before women received the right to vote in 1920.

Ryan quickly went to work learning more about Parkhurst's fascinating story. Ryan blended ideas from her imagination with facts about Parkhurst's life.

At first, Ryan planned to tell Parkhurst's story in a picture book. Then, her editor suggested that a longer book would be better. In 1998, *Riding Freedom* was published. The book was Ryan's first novel. It earned the **California Young Reader Medal**.

Ryan continued to write historical fiction about courageous women. *Amelia and Eleanor Go for a Ride* is a story about Amelia Earhart and Eleanor Roosevelt.

In Ryan's book, Earhart takes Roosevelt for an airplane ride over Washington, D.C. Later, Roosevelt takes Earhart for a ride in her car. In 2000, the book was named an **American Library Association (ALA)** Notable Book.

Earhart (left) was the first woman pilot to fly alone across the Atlantic Ocean. Roosevelt (right) was First Lady, the wife of President Franklin Delano Roosevelt.

Esperanza's Story

As a child, Ryan heard her grandmother Esperanza's stories about life in the farm camps. Later, Ryan learned that her grandmother's family had been wealthy in Mexico. Yet, Esperanza left that life behind when she moved to the United States.

Inspired by her grandmother's story, Ryan wove one of her own. *Esperanza Rising* is the story of a wealthy young girl from Mexico. Esperanza Ortega has fine clothes and servants. Then her father is killed.

Esperanza and her mother flee Mexico. In California, they have little choice but to hire themselves out picking fruit. The story tells how Esperanza deals with her change in fortune and overcomes new challenges.

In 2002, *Esperanza Rising* earned the **ALA**'s **Pura Belpré Award**. The ALA also named it one of the top ten best books of the year for young adults. *Esperanza Rising* later became a play. Theater groups across the country performed it.

Also in 2002, *When Marian Sang* was published. This book is about the life of talented African-American singer Marian Anderson. She was denied many opportunities simply because she was not white. In 2003, *When Marian Sang* was named an **ALA Robert F. Sibert Honor Book**.

Then in 2004, *Becoming Naomi León* took readers on a journey from California to Mexico. The novel is the story of a girl named Naomi and her younger brother, Owen. They live with their great-grandmother, who they call Gram.

After abandoning them years earlier, Naomi's mother suddenly appears and wants to reclaim Naomi. In order to protect the children, Gram takes Naomi and Owen to Mexico to find their father. *Becoming Naomi León* was named a **Pura Belpré Honor Book** in 2006.

Marian Anderson

Full-Time Writer

Ryan's writing success has allowed her to be a full-time writer. Today, she has a studio in her home. The writing life can be very different from working in an office! Ryan has no coworkers to talk with during the day. However, she also has no long commute.

Usually, Ryan begins a new book with a trip to the library for research. Her job is a lot like writing a paper for school. First, she collects information. Then, she puts it all together.

Ryan prefers to do most of her writing in the morning. She begins her books with a rough **draft**. Then, she continues to work on the draft until she is happy with it. Ryan estimates she may **revise** a story or a novel between 20 and 30 times!

Not all of Ryan's **manuscripts** become published books. There are manuscripts she has stopped working on. Sometimes, she will start over on one. It takes a lot of time and effort to craft a good book.

Ryan spends about two years researching and writing her novels.

New Experiences, New Books

Today, Ryan lives in Leucadia, California. Her home is near the Pacific Ocean. When she is not working, Ryan likes to read, travel, and watch movies. She also takes walks on the beach. Recently, she has learned to ride horses.

Ryan began taking riding lessons while researching her latest book. Her research took her to many places and brought her many new experiences. She recalls one six-hour ride in driving rain! Still another time, she and her horse were caught for hours in a swarm of biting, buzzing flies.

All of these experiences helped her write *Paint the Wind*. Ryan's latest book is about another young woman's challenges. *Paint the Wind* tells the story of an orphan named Maya and a wild horse named Artemisia. Like many of Ryan's books, it blends adventure, a courageous female character, and the importance of family.

Opposite page: *Ryan loved horses as a child. However, she had few opportunities to be with them. Today, she is able to ride often!*

Pam Muñoz Ryan continues to delight readers with well-researched, engaging stories. She wants kids to love books and reading as much as she did. Her award-winning books will make that an easy goal to reach!

Glossary

American Library Association (ALA) - an organization that promotes the highest quality library and information services and public access to information.

California Young Reader Medal - awarded by California's children to an original work of fiction published within the last four years by a living author.

degree - a title given by a college to its graduates after they have completed their studies.

draft - an early version or outline.

gender - behavioral, societal, and mental elements that are commonly associated with one sex.

genre - a type of art, music, or literature that follows a particular style, form, or content.

Great Depression - the period from 1929 to 1942 of worldwide economic trouble when there was little buying or selling, and many people could not find work.

manuscript - a book or an article written by hand or typed before being published.

persevere - to continue steadily on a course of action in spite of difficulties or obstacles.

Pura Belpré Award - presented to a Latino or Latina writer and illustrator whose work best portrays, affirms, and celebrates the Latino cultural experience in an outstanding work of literature for children and youth. Selected runners-up are called Pura Belpré Honor Books.

revise - to change something in order to correct or improve it.

Robert F. Sibert Medal - awarded annually to the author and illustrator of the most distinguished informational book published in English during the preceding year. Selected runners-up are called Robert F. Sibert Honor Books.

Web Sites

To learn more about Pam Muñoz Ryan, visit ABDO Publishing Company on the World Wide Web at **www.abdopublishing.com**. Web sites about Pam Muñoz Ryan are featured on our Book Links page. These links are routinely monitored and updated to provide the most current information available.

Index